Storm

Written by Anthony Masters
Illustrated by Philippe Dupasquier

Heinemann

Chapter 1

Matt and Katie were on holiday. Every year their parents rented the same holiday cottage. It was on the cliffs, high above a little Cornish bay. Matt and Katie loved going to the seaside.

This year Dad had bought them a dinghy and had promised he would teach them both how to row. Matt had already had a few lessons and he really enjoyed it.

'You two can go ahead down to the beach,' said Dad, 'but don't get in the boat until we get there. I'll bring the oars as they're a bit tricky to carry. Mum will bring the life-jackets.'

'I'll just finish getting the picnic ready,' said Mum, 'and then we'll join you on the beach. Don't forget – you're not to go in the boat until Dad and I arrive!'

Matt and Katie carried their dinghy down the long, winding path to the beach. The sea was calm and it was quite sunny, but there were a few grey clouds in the sky.

'Is it going to rain?' asked Katie.

'I hope not,' said Matt, noticing the clouds. He was looking forward to another rowing lesson with Dad. Katie hadn't been very interested in learning how to row yet. But Matt knew it was only a matter of time before she insisted on having lessons too.

When they got down to the beach, Katie said, 'I'm sure it's okay if we just put the boat in the water.'

'No!' said Matt. 'Mum and Dad said we have to wait for them.'

'Please, Matt!' begged Katie. 'We can just float about in the shallow water.'

'Dad and Mum told us to wait,' repeated Matt.

But Katie was already running down to the sea, dragging the dinghy behind her. 'We'll be all right, Matt. We can just sit in the boat until Mum and Dad get here.'

Matt sighed and looked out across the calm sea. In the distance, he could see Gull Rock, glinting in the sunshine.

Last year Katie and he had gone with Mum and Dad on a boat ride to see Gull Rock. It had looked exciting from the speed boat, but then the captain told them about the strong currents that swept round Gull Rock. He said many boats had been wrecked there in the past. After that Matt was quite glad to see Gull Rock from the safety of the shore.

When Matt looked back at Katie, she was dragging the dinghy into the gentle waves that were breaking on the sand. He was going to call out to her to come back. Then, he thought maybe there was no harm in just sitting in the dinghy, in the shallow water.

He looked round for a big stone. 'Hang on, Katie,' he yelled.

'What?' called Katie.

'Give me the rope. I'm going to put this heavy stone on it so the boat can't drift off.'

'Okay. Hurry up then,' said Katie.

Matt and Katie got into the dinghy, which was bobbing up and down in the shallow water. Matt enjoyed the sound of the water that was gently rocking the dinghy.

Matt looked along the beach. There were no other people there. He tried to see if Mum and Dad were on their way down the path, but there was no sign of them. A seagull was flying back to its nest near the top of the cliff. Katie was busy trailing her hand in the water, catching clumps of seaweed, and Matt day-dreamed.

Neither of them noticed that the dinghy was drifting gently away from the shore. Then Katie suddenly shouted, 'Look, Matt! The rope has come away from the stone!'

Matt saw the end of the rope,
floating in the water. Then he looked
down into the dark water. The sea
was much too deep. He wouldn't be
able to jump in and pull the dinghy
back to the shore.

As he looked round, he heard a
rumble of thunder and just at that
moment, the sun disappeared behind
a big, dark cloud.

Chapter 2

'What are we going to do now?'
Katie's voice trembled. Matt could
see she was frightened.

   'I don't know,' he said, trying hard
not to show how scared he was. 'Dad
must get down here soon. He was
going to bring the oars.' Then Matt
remembered something that made
him feel sick — Mum had the
life-jackets!

'You should have fixed the rope better,' moaned Katie.

'And you should have waited for Mum and Dad – like they said!' shouted Matt.

Katie had been clever, as usual, in getting her own way, but Matt knew he would get the blame for getting in the dinghy. He felt miserable and couldn't think what to do.

The dinghy kept on drifting and the waves were getting bigger all the time.

'Help!' yelled Matt. 'Help!' But there was no one around to hear his cries.

'Help!' screamed Katie, at the top of her voice. 'Someone help us! Please!'

The dinghy had drifted out from the calm water of the bay and the waves were much bigger now. Dark clouds raced across the sky. The seagulls swooped low, making wild cries, as if warning Katie and Matt that they were drifting into terrible danger.

'I'm frightened,' said Katie.

'Don't worry,' said Matt. 'Mum and Dad are bound to come down to the beach soon. They'll know what to do.'

But Katie began to sob.

The wind was coming in strong gusts and the dinghy was being pushed out towards the open sea. The drizzling rain soon became a downpour.

Katie's cries grew louder.

'Stop crying, Katie. I think I can hear something,' said Matt.

The wind was so noisy that they had to listen hard. They could hear, in the distance, the chugging sound of a fishing boat engine.

'Come on, Katie! Shout for help!' yelled Matt.

The two children shouted as loudly as they could, but their voices were lost in the strong wind.

Matt began to wave wildly, but the dinghy rocked dangerously from side to side.

Katie screamed, 'Matt! Sit down! You're going to tip the boat over!' Matt sat down again.

'It's no good, Katie. The fishing boat hasn't seen us,' he said, grimly.

The two children watched, feeling miserable, as the fishing boat disappeared into the misty darkness.

'What's going to happen to us?' cried Katie.

Matt didn't know. All he could think of was how worried Mum and Dad would be when they reached the beach and found that Katie and he had disappeared.

Then Katie cried out, 'Oh, no! Look Matt!' She stared ahead, horrified.

Matt looked over his shoulder and saw that their dinghy was heading straight for Gull Rock. As Matt and Katie watched, a flash of lightning lit up the steep sides of Gull Rock, and there was a loud clap of thunder overhead.

'We're going to drown!' cried Katie, and she crouched down in the dinghy.

'Don't worry, Katie. Someone will help us,' said Matt. But he knew she wouldn't believe him. Why should she? The fishing boat hadn't seen them.

As the dinghy drifted nearer Gull Rock, Matt and Katie could hear a horrible booming sound as the waves crashed on to the great rock.

Gull Rock had seemed exciting when they saw it on a calm day last year, but in the storm it looked terrifying – rising out of the rain and spray like a gigantic, towering castle.

'We're going to crash into Gull Rock!' screamed Katie.

Matt wasn't listening. He was looking round to see if there was any place they could land on Gull Rock. Then he spotted a ledge, sticking out above the waves. Matt knew that if they could get on to that ledge, they might be safer.

'Come on, Katie! You've got to help me!' said Matt. 'We'll have to paddle the boat with our hands.'

'I can't,' said Katie. 'I want Mummy.'

'Look, Katie,' said Matt, 'it's our only chance. We have to get to that ledge, there,' he said, pointing. 'We might be able to jump on to it.'

Chapter 3

Desperately, Katie and Matt paddled the dinghy towards the ledge.

'Get ready to jump,' said Matt, and he grabbed Katie's hand. 'One, two, three, JUMP!' yelled Matt.

Amazingly, they both landed on the ledge. Katie grabbed hold of the rock and hung on, but Matt slipped on the wet surface and slid back into the sea.

Katie shrank back against the rock. Then she saw Matt's head, bobbing up and down in the surf. She watched him swim towards the ledge and grab a huge clump of seaweed. He pulled at it, trying to scramble on to the ledge, but his hands were too cold and stiff to hold on.

A wave threw Matt against the
rock. Katie was horrified to see
blood streaming down her brother's
face. He managed to grab the
seaweed again, but he couldn't pull
himself up on to the rock.

Katie was scared but she knew
she had to help Matt. She leaned
over the ledge. 'Grab my hand!'
she shouted.

With a great effort, Matt reached up and struggled to reach Katie's hand. At that moment, Matt's feet found a small ridge of rock that was buried by the swirling sea. He gripped it with his feet and flung himself forward. Katie grabbed the back of his T-shirt and pulled him on to the ledge. He lay there, gasping and panting.

After a few minutes, Matt sat up and looked out to sea. The wind was blowing hard and the waves were huge. He glanced at Katie, who looked terrified.

'The storm's getting worse,' he thought. 'The waves are going to drag us back into the sea.'

Suddenly, they heard a loud noise in the sky. Matt and Katie both looked up. At first they couldn't see through the rain and clouds. Then they saw a big helicopter hovering right above them. Matt and Katie waved and shouted, screaming at the top of their voices.

'The helicopter has come to rescue us!' cried Matt.

They watched as a man was lowered slowly down towards them. The man landed on the rock and put an arm round Katie.

'It's okay, you're safe now,' he said. He put Katie into a harness. 'Don't worry, son, I'll be back for you in a minute!' he shouted to Matt.

Matt could hardly believe they were being rescued.

He waved to the man. Just then a huge wave swept over the ledge and washed Matt into the sea.

Matt was so weak that he could hardly swim and the water dragged him away from the ledge.

Matt gazed up hopefully into the sky.

He saw the man on the helicopter cable, hovering above him.

'Don't worry, son! I'll have you out of the sea in no time!' he called to Matt. The next moment, Matt felt the man's strong arms putting him into the safety of the harness. 'Having a quick swim, were you?' joked the man.

Soon they were being lifted into the safety of the helicopter. Matt looked down and thought he saw the remains of the dinghy – torn to pieces on the jagged rocks.

'That could have been Katie and me,' he thought.

Once Matt was safely aboard the helicopter, he was wrapped in a blanket just like Katie's.

The man said to Matt, 'Your mum and dad will be thrilled to see you safe and sound. It was a really stupid thing, getting into the dinghy without them, but I expect you've learned your lesson.'

Matt looked at Katie. She nodded at him.

'We certainly have!' he said.